NOTH
TAKEN
ULTIMAT
ABOUT THE WORLD HAS NOT YET BEEN
SPOKEN THE WORLD IS OPEN AND FREE
EVERYTHING IS STILL IN THE FUTURE AND
WILL ALWAYS BE

NOTHING CONCLUSIVE
HAS YET TAKEN PLACE IN THE
WORLD THE ULTIMATE WORD
OF THE WORLD AND ABOUT
THE WORLD HAS NOT YET BEEN
SPOKEN THE WORLD IS OPEN
AND FREE EVERYTHING IS STILL
IN THE FUTURE AND WILL
ALWAYS BE

TIM ATKINS

Crater Press
63

Crater 63
The Crater Press
Kennington | Mataró | New Malden | Constanta

ISBN 978-1-008-99478-2
First Published 2021

All images by Tim Atkins
Book design & typesetting by Koshifuri Ices

The title of this book is from
Bakhtin's "Problems of Dostoevsky's Poetics"

With thanks to the editors of the following publications in which
versions of these poems first appeared: *the 87press, Tentacular,
Pamenar, Blackbox Manifold, Sulfur Surrealist Jungle.*

20th Century font was designed and drawn by Sol Hess in the
Lanston Monotype drawing office between 1936 and 1947. The
first weights were added to the Monotype typeface library in
1959. This is a face based on geometric shapes which originated
in Germany in the early 1920s and became an integral part of
the Bauhaus movement of that time.

This book consists of original poems and translations of the
work of the following poets: Osip Mandelstam, Marina Tsvetaeva,
Nazim Hikmet, Mayakovsky, Ovid, et al

Written:
New Malden Summer 2018
Boulder Colorado Fall 2019 *While on an international artist's
residency at The Boulder Museum of Contemporary Art.
With thanks*
Covid 2020
Brexit 2021

Tristia | The Black Sea | Little Britain

CONTENTS

This book is for Chiaki Koto Yuki

& their children

& their children

Let no light through your window.

        Keep your body concealed.

            The game is up.

               Ovid

Perhaps there is a life here

Of not being afraid of your own heart beating

Do not be afraid of your own heart beating

Look at very small things with your eyes

& stay warm

Nothing outside can cure you but everything's outside

There is great shame for the world in knowing

You may have gone this far

Perhaps this is why you love the presence of other people so much

Perhaps this is why you wait so impatiently

You have nothing more to teach

Until there is no more panic at the knowledge of your own real
    existence

& then only special childish laughter to be shown

& no more lies no more

Not to find you no

More coming back & more returning

Southern journey

Small things & not my own debris

               Bernadette Mayer

If you put it in a book and send it

If you put it in a book
And send it out
If you put it in a book in order to resist
If you wrote that book from under your bed
If you wrote that book because you could not sleep
Because they used to rip only the arms off
You put it in a book and send it out or
If the sea is black or if it is always filled with people or
 ice
You put it in a book called *Tristia* (this)
Because you are and the letters and the book
Play the role of your beloved and of your servant
And you send it out for 2000 years and you send it out
Thinking that somebody is needing to read it
Even if you cannot bring yourself to get out from under
 the bed
In order to change the world
You and clean or cleaner clothes
If the bed is some kind of comfort or if you put it in a
 book
And you cannot think who is ever going to read it who
 is left
In Rome who is still reading or eating or living or
 smoking even
Who is reading or sleeping or leaving the house
Going out to watch contact sports instead of reading
 the book
You would maybe send out if you wrote it

In order to resist you say you will write it to resist if you
    can write it
Because you would rather be sleep or you would rather
    be sex
In a book about thinking about power and how to be
    small
Or invisible in order to exist like dust does a whole
    book of it
Made up of dead dusts which you have lived in
The dead white male poet role
In exile from the academy because it was and you are
    doomed
In order to exist like an artist without hope and/or
    money
Beside the black sea and great hope
No money and dust if you put it down in a book
And get round to sending it out
It turns on your thoughts of the empire
In order to be small or invisible again so that you can
    move
Instead of thinking about writing a book
Sadness and the black sea letters a final book of
    insults and spells it was
A dark and stormy night then and it is again and I think
    of the gods
Who are no longer gods or the gods are just tools
Stuck into the idea of the book of the west
Studying hunger I season its concept
With noting my anger something my anger is
A book anger it always has and I don't send it out
I look at cucumbers in a wan light

I think about all the small poems that I used to send out
Letters saying *your language is weak* and even
Ooh la la! I was a bad artist and I was a boring one
When I send my books out in order to resist
Ageing pollution men bikes and
Dicks it is good to think about
Paper and the size and the shape of things books sent
out or not
Sent out in order to resist staying in inside the house
breathing dust
You make a list of modes of resistance
Consisting of phrasal verbs and adjectives
You want a book made of nylon to repel dampness
If the sea is black or if it is always filled with people or
plastics
The seas filled with mountains of plastic the sun
Burning the bodies piled high on those islands
Breaking up in the sun streaked white where the birds
shit
On the pink and blue black plastic bodies tossed
wrappers into the sea
The wine dark sea of wet wipes and ghosts Algerians
Moroccans etcetras
And you cannot build a wall against the water
Just the same as you cannot build
A book anger which you may well send out
If you can locate your arms or the lost bits of kids
If you can get through their cages if they do not hold
them under
The boiling cold sea

What will the world do with your book if you write it
    and send it out
Listing numbers but numbers if you can imagine them
    drowning in a black water
Filled with plastics out there an island or mountain
One there of bottles and one there of bodies
One then a site of habitation and the other of nutrition
What does it taste like to a fish or a sea bird to eat
The floating parts of an Algerian from the mountains or
A coast dweller from the coast or the tiny parts of a
    family
Possibly sub-Saharan
From your position in exile
Beneath a bed in a small town beside the Black Sea
    resisting
This volume which
You will or will not
Ever move to send out

When I look around me everything has been broken or stolen

When I look around me and the eyes go into the world
To caress objects in order to feel something
It is like a night on a boat that you do not want to be in
Because your legs cannot make it
You notice that your book is constructed of mainly body
    parts
Yours failing but moving
The others always out there in your mind in the night
Because you can feel them taking tiny bites out of the
American empire also European and dumb
Russian and you think that your book
Existed to help them if they or it really existed
If there was someone to read it you once knew
A woman could make such an appeal
Because nothing exists in the way that an army does or
    an ideology
Alone or together upon a flat or undulating surface
Acting against the gods Caesar green floods sound
    poetry and logging
I do not fear death because
I have lived in the thought of a boat or a book
    not received but sent out goes by pending in surprise
A fly lands on my arm as if to prove something
And another fly comes and wants to get off
In the air on a boat in the middle of night
But the air will not let it you cannot
Move like that because you are only pretending to be
    alive

Or an insect suffering memory loss
Concerning the time when you had control
Over the men and women of genre fiction
You suck their things knowing how to start them or stop
On a bridge cantilever suspension arch cable stayed
    beam or truss
The sexual act described with reference to flowers and
    donkeys
It is hard to fit everything into this bed or this boat
When I think of you I look up and see my writing
Imbued with insecurity destabilization heartbreak
    longing and bitterness
Looking at the exit in the shape
Of an aid to psychological counselling on subways at
    parties
Etc. using colored pens to color-code emotions
A workable code or shorthand
For the transcription of every event motion and
    transition
In order to render several effects of banishment
Such as changed status for both self and new writing
Remorse for having written things
Fear deference fear of dying away and apologies
The identity of exile and of writer
How they are incompatible
Now the house is charred
Now the house has been emptied out
Now the house when the book and the house which
    never moves
And the house which loses concentration
And the smart bombs

Identify many roles for this volume
The dead hats all thrown out into the park off the
   beach
Their head space assimilated and identified in roles
   such as
Slave messenger mourner intercessor child
When the exiled poet refers to birthing or noting or
   killing their work
Beneath the sea in the search for pencils
Legs dogs cats fish pigeons ducks rats snakes
Work stations eyeglasses hearing device prosthetics
Thesaurus children subordinates chapstik blutak
Viagra embodiment passion concentration and supreme
   authority
With fixed purpose
Pointing towards liberation and escape
I imagine what it is like not to be myself not to be
Not looking from the Black Sea up at Stalingrad across
   the endless steppe
Across time at the dirty concrete
Noting the dead
Books ripped off how phenomena appear to unfold
   boldly
Failing and incomplete
I imagine what it is like to be a poet and it is good
   wearing clothes
I imagine being in a room full of men declaiming their
   sound poetry
Each attempting to make their audience feel the
   greater discomfort
My dream what

Was a dream of beauty
No more self-harm or pursuit
You stand up to address the audience and you say
This is my new book and this is its title
All in caps on the cover
The time has come in the dream
To smell the coffee
For this is the first noble truth
How shit life is and shit you must
At this moment in
History—all over
The master discourse

You make an appeal and

You make an appeal to whoever because
You make an appeal to whoever because you do not
  get what you want
Because you do not get what you want
From your position under the bed beside the wine dark
  sea
And under its blackness the black
Coming because it has absorbed all of your night
Or because the wine dark sea is not liquor but blood
  the
Blood of the ass and the eye and the ear and the nose
And the car and door and the arm and apartment
  filling up
You make an appeal because when you make an
  appeal
You can write it and writing perhaps is an indication of
  power
When you do not have any beside the bed beside the
  door beside the light beside the sea
And everything says that your power has gone and you
  are living on a place
That has been abandoned and besieged and to
  escape you know you must
Call favour from the nameless ones who have been
  holding a small dog up to your face
And squeezing it till it squirts because they can
And you put them in your book and you tell them it is a
  good book and the book is

You assure them waterproof because it is made of
  nylon and it is not and you
Move your body like this and like that practising how
  you would do things
If you ever were to appear again before them
  scraping yourself
Beside the wine dark sea which is frozen in high
  summer in the heat in the night
Pressing down upon you from your position under your
  bed the zone
Known for earthquakes along the coasts barbarian
  raids and racists in capes
Who you could resist if only you had proof of their
  existence in this book
In the real world going out into the eyes of real
  readers and real words
In an unreal world in which your powers are fading
  beside your genius
Of the sea which is impossible to look at from your
  position
Bent double from scraping in order to appear servile
To give service to humans or books
Writing bent double from the position of vitamin loss
Such as the ones that seeped out when you were
  making love and not loved
And the ones which you lost mostly b vitamins
When you wasted your time watching the conductors of
  chaos writing erotic verse
Slowly noticing the advance of the new confessional
Feeling sad by the side of the sea eating wings and
  chilli or legs and BBQ sauce

It would be good to become reconciled to the
    ascendancy of the
Poseurs and line managers that surround you at night
From your position beneath the bed with insomnia and
    the dust
Pushing them away with an imaginary book
It would be good to repeat the line about no suffering
    and no self
And it would be good to be drinking a hot or cold
    drink
In the same way that it would be good to be making
    love
To a woman or a man or an animal on a table or shelf
    space
Telling you that you are if not alive then a genius
And that you still have some kind of occult
Power over words the way that many possess over food
In their ability to procure cook and consume it
You are a middle-aged author by the edge of a black
    sea
And you are no longer welcome in the academy for
    good reason
Or upon the Charing Cross Road because you are
Angry white and entitled
And you have been since the invention of the penis in
    Mesopotamia
And you do not know this is good
Although it is just because
Your world has the taste that a worm gets
As it moves through your books

And when you are writing this poem

And when you are writing this poem and you are
  travelling
And the point of this thing is that you are in the middle
  of it
Even when you are no longer in the middle of it
Nouning and thinking about your life you have opinions
Your watch is slipping around on your wrist
Because you are unstable on uneven ground wet
  surfaces or boats in cities
It is different
To hold on to the arm of a friend or to lean upon walls
Unless they are too hot as is often the case in the
  capitol but
You thought for a long time
You thought you were impervious and it was easy to
  kiss or be kissed
You thought that only wheels needed lubricant or doors
Once upon a time everybody wanted to have sex
And the proof was on film with all your friends there in
  a doorway
Or up against a wall in an apartment or in an
  illustrated book
And when you were writing that poem
It was the equivalent of spending something
Moving like fishes in the metaphor for the poem one
  line leading on
You now see
Inevitably towards cliché not the literary type but the
  one imagined

By the rebel or the revolutionary in a reactionary
    landscape
And the eye can leave the body when it finds
The truly beloved's systems of belief
And the eye can leave the body when it finds a sloppy
    or poor torturer
(Unless disfigurement is the aim) if that game is a kiss
You are or you were on a boat listing
And your illness is displacement and there is no lintel or
    wall friend or wife
Every time your line reaches across for the right side of
    the page it fails because
The life of a writer inclines
And the life of a poet inclines towards repetition
Thoughts being like photos that you cannot think
    through to connect
One book about something and the next about another
And then it just gets to the third being the same as the
    first
And the second the same as the fourth
Your growing recognition leading to self-loathing and
    respect
Now that you are famous or human enough
To be covered with marble cracks
A small area of explanation appears on the horizon
Sealing over the thought of you to resist penetration
There are half birds hoodless and buses the author
    come upon a bear pattern
And your image goes out
You do not know any longer if this is the middle of a
    nightmare or the middle of the night

There are two cats and a jellyfish corn size at the
    beach
The appeals that you make to friends all disappear
Because there is no coverage here
The sea sucks the waves down to no bars or battery
    left
You smoke and you smoke and the signals you breathe
    in you breathe out
If anybody could read them
They would say this
You thought you were a good character
When you were in somebody else's books
Your friendship or the history of surrealism being a
    dilution of dada
In the way that most writing works worse
With one single X-chromosome instead of the double X
You are writing about abnormalities occurring upon the
    sea
Being a statistic
Black in a footnote
And black being the colour of what it says about life
In a line called a life until either runs out
You are in a boat on a bed in the sea in your mind in a
    part of your life on the Romanian east coast
And all you want to do is put your head between
Anyone's legs
And stop being you
If you can stop being you
You don't care what they do

There was a time you thought

There was a time you thought you lived with them and
   you knew what to do
Mornings easy to wake up inside things like peaches
The Righteous Brothers
Sweet and soft not bruised because it was easy to
   handle them gently
Round and good colours when pressed close to the
   nose
How long do these things ever last if you strip the
   detail out
If you reduce a human to their essence perhaps you
   find a calendar and
Perhaps for an instant you do not hate the smell of gas
The history of it being human
The history of renewing the body and the song to avoid
   it
In a book called *The History of Shit*
You can remember the taste of it upon Frank Sinatra
And the smell of the gas
Playing in the mornings when we are talking
That was when you lived with them
And there was a time you can remember writing about
   it
Which has passed from your position beneath the bed
When you are stoned and alone
There was a time when the water came all the way up
   to the shore
There was a time when I was you and she was me and I
   was neither you nor them

The fingers there sometime good inside and sometimes
    out
Making love you thought involving a basic vocabulary
So that it could be used to give pleasure and at the
    same time
To overthrow the government
Your erogenous zones arrayed with fresh cherries
How good it would be to overthrow the government
By writing about how to overthrow it
This is the mode of the poets
After and before making love in a bed in a book but
    you know
You always want things you can't have or don't got
You thought you were taking photographs of the
    beloved
Asleep on a lake on a boat and looking beneath
    seeing the green and grey fish
Do they sleep for how long inside it after making love
The water the fish the feeling and the sleep
The boat and the human
And the world and the book
This thought and what happens to it

Because reading is an excuse for real life you read things

Because reading is an excuse for having a personality
    or social grace
It is good to burn your old books
However many remain
Piled high in the corridors and corners
Ugly white men to remind us
That everything we invented was wrong
Wanking over each other's collected works
While every time that you write is an attempt to
    escape
Through the application of right speech
In your life everywhere there is evidence of writing and
    there is evidence of reading
In your presence my front is not felt
I can't feel my face when I'm with you
Because when we write we write alone
It is important to return to scraping sometimes to go
    back home
You know how often you have failed in books to
    practice right speech
You lack sincerity you did the same on Second Avenue
You wrote personism in less than ten thousand seconds
Nobody comes looking for a poet unless they are a
    bad one
Which you can prove from your prizes and press when
    you were famous
In the papers there is a column listing daily outrages
And at dawn we took a bath together and read the
    poets

Ovid that did not help when they can smell the
    Blackshirts
It would have been so much better to stick to elegies
Because reading down the centre of the page without
    moving your eyes
Is a kind of grace which is a warning from the capitol
    concerning human rights
It would have been better to expend your energies
    upon silence maybe some
Licking and product placement
The undersea world of Jacques Cousteau
His breathing apparatus adventures and beautiful
    squid to whom
You were mansplaining at the front of this book
Concerning the death of the author but who wrote it
Perhaps you have dreamed of being kissed in a
    foreign language
And dreamed of being invisible and dreamed of being
    free
All you have is this list
And this list is your poetics
Yo soy marinero! Yo no soy capitan!
Nothing holy! Vast emptiness!

In The Art of Love you make things up

Because it is impossible not to
But now there is nothing left of you
That makes sense
Nobody likes you for it and
You are all things to all people
That you cannot erase or write out
Everything is a piece of time in which
The phallus poses for us
It is manifestly imaginary
And must be stepped on
This surplus jouissance
And you know that
A woman can use others' art
Far better in your defence
And that they can take from it
Without being taught and
You remember Praxilla
In your book Petrarch
Her line about cucumbers
It being your favourite
And the stars when the men
Called her stupid
You gasped then
You read up on hair types
And you think about how often you have looked
You have examined the plastic arts
And found them confusing
And you have looked at forests and at fields
And they make your eyes water

And it is true that you have failed
To stop writing about cucumbers and grow them
When you have failed to stop thinking about love
You lift up your head and these systems are long
    forgotten
In the circus they whip animals and then
Take pictures of them with women and men
Shimmering with moustaches and the animals
Their love of a smoke huddling together
Outside portacabins in the dusk or the dazzling light
While the bird boys kiss parrots' heads and tilt towards
    love
Their tiny white feathers sticking in the dusk to dark lips
You go to the circus to feel something
And it makes everything black
Some return with certificates
Explaining that they have earned the right to
Explain things most notably men
Blood going from parts
You are at the circus
And you would rather be at the carnival
The noise of chaos is better than the screaming of
    animals
Clowns bearded women in sequins
And the male gaze makes you sick
You are walking towards the sea wall
You think everything you say will take you down
Further than everyone you have ever known out of
    knowing it
And further down than everything
Before you can say anything

The book rises up in the night
You knew it was coming
And perhaps there is too much explanation
You have problems with shoes and then with
    conjunctions
At this point in the new millennium your new poem
Is a list of errors erasures and apologies
And that perhaps is its strong point
But if you are wrong
It is just a list of non-sequiturs and false starts
Lines of varying power and irregular length
Gestures towards invisible or impossible beings
Weak appeals and mistakes

When you see a dead body you write

When you see a dead body you write about life
And then afterwards
Simplicity no conflict and rectitude
Tranquilized in the foreground
How hard is it to move something on a planet with
    cancer
Mankind and in summer every day
You can go out and watch them killing
Black boys walking home on summer lawns
And young women in schools
You learned virtually nothing in
And all summer you weep
Working with certain modes of discourse
Whose advancement depends entirely upon certain
    events
That at key moments in the illocutionary situation
    trigger a new flow of speech
Nazim Hikmet wrote *Remember a prisoner's beloved*
    must always think beautiful thoughts
When downloading texts concerning the end of the
    world
Lying helps when you look at a corpse
Every day in the papers emotion eludes the subject
In the London Hilton
You expect something from a man
But you were wrong about either the man or the
    weather
You do not expect to be betrayed by the living or the
    dead

Only because you do not expect anything
When standing by the dog track in the dusk looking up
There was a moment
And all you can see are apartments filled with people
   arguing
Covered with sweat some choosing soft furnishings and
   orange lights
Others blue more or white light different for effect
   from the table or ceiling
There is some dust from the track on your losing ticket
   silhouette
Which you are breathing all in to the lower zones to
   replenish the kidney
Remembering everything like rumours in poems to be in
   and strive again
Row upon row of imaginary lovers standing in front of
   the usual water
Wearing gloves to handle doorknobs in Buster Keaton
One man hits another with a fist or a candle or lawsuit
We kissed each other on the lips to say something to
   men and we kissed each other as humans do in front
   of municipal structures
Once we were workers in the culture industry
Contributing to the gross national product but
Kissing I did not ask you to bite my lips and you did
When you see a dead body remember when you eat a
   dead body
It could be yours
Be sure to check the sell-by date
If you lack a spine
Or a swarm of flies rise

When Walter Jackson sings "Welcome Home"

When Walter Jackson sings "Welcome Home" in 1965
In black and white
And he casts off his crutches
When he does this and you watch him
You watch him in the corner of a room and it is
Almost as if he is living and you are still smoking
Perhaps he has received Jesus in the world he grew up
   in
And perhaps he grew up in his head in his church
And perhaps he knows better
That you are godless and appealing to be taken
Back or taken up or taken in
In spite of the brownouts
Staring out at the set
You realize how badly you require salvation
A soul review to take part in or watch one on a bus
Driving out of the Carpathian Mountains pulling up
The men and women tired and hungry
Walking in to a diner only hopeful of getting attention
Because there are racists the plains and in the
   mountains
You check your privilege and having checked it
The problem is that you cannot go forward in time or
   backwards
You say that you can
In the imagination or in books
But everyone still acts the same and the toxins
Still get dumped in the seas and the rivers and the
   streams

Not to mention fly tipping and all you can do is
Sign a petition to resist agribusiness but
Your digital signature means nothing to a Viking
When the Vikings pull in and do whatever appeals say
Fracking the fixing of juries with gangsters or murder
You have seen them in operation
In poetry competitions
You thought you were the obvious winner
But you weren't Viking enough for someone perhaps
You think your writing was better when
All the references to sex sounded ambiguous
Or written by young men or young women
Or appealing as opposed to sleazy or obscene
Age makes you sick when you look at yourself
But you tell yourself that your audience once
Approved of your small songs of love
The ones in which people
Crawled in and all over each other
Without giving out or being given up
And you thought all you ever wanted was this
But now you live in a cold water apartment
With Walter Johnson and
Your digital signature no longer works
In the parts when you click
It is always too late and it is never too late
To summon all the tall and the beautiful ones
To come and give comfort call Jesus and sing
The stylus settling in to its bed of black vinyl
The ear
Finding the horns
Before reaching the strings

In Catalunya upon the Costa Brava

Women piss into the water at dawn
When a fishing boat sets out
To send it good luck for the men there departing
The strong and the hairy ones
The way you left Rome too
On a sea of brutality and piss
On a day in the past into exile long before you
    remember
The having or the absence of luck
In the mornings it was good to eat pancakes with
    blueberries
And butter and maple syrup and finishing
Leave puddles on the side of the plate
In Jane Austen the novelist remains oblivious
To the ones who you thought of as servants
Though when the world went on
You visited the king of the gypsies in Paris then
At the end of the war
But you would have hated it
Getting on a bus
In Austria and Vienna and in Paris
You could sink your teeth into a lover's neck
Surrounded by engine noise and exhausts
Drawing positions and instructions in notebooks upon
    independence
They do things differently in Catalunya
And in other semi-autonomous regions then
One day in the Roman Empire you wake up on a boat
    and there are men

Your name is Ovid and all that remains to you is to
    write notes
Upon the Cyclades and the Pleiades
Because it is your purpose to notice these things
As a sensitive artist
In the absence of trees and
If there are people in the sea in the night
You would not be able to see them
Perhaps because you are a little short-sighted
From an excess of sex
But you can hear them and feel them
Not every artist comes up hard against an empire the
    way you do
When you realise that the moment in which you are
    alive is a time
When you are finished culturally and historically
You do not believe you are beyond anything
New poetry and poetics from which you are sailing but
At last you think yes
It must be good to be old and good to be gone
If you want to give up
Your star sign indicates problems with the heart
And that makes sense being born in August
Surrounded by the heat and the dust
You think of the ones who could save you
But it is too late now you think of the things you said
About their native weather
And the state of their chapbooks
You do not regret your vomit landing upon Philip and
    Ted
Because they were bores at a party once

Somewhere in Oakland just like you
Knowing nothing of women and little of men
Poets compromised in their ability to rap
In Rome and all capitols
They were holding your arms ostensibly to steady you
And there were other men holding your arms
Ostensibly to keep you upright
But they were gripping too tight
Beneath the black sky turning bright
And you seasick at the sight
Privilege is something you all had in common and it was
    useful
Until the juice all seeped out
You realise that you could have saved yourself a long
    time ago
Because it is something that anyone can do
If you go back in time far enough
Until you land on a boat
And there are bodies on top of bodies on top of other
    bodies
Banjo and accordion players and sous-chefs and
    doctors and cooks
Being pushed off
You realise you could have saved yourself if you had
    given up
Everything writing and sex
But you could never give up
And every time you feel the boat pitch
It pushes your face underneath
Your empire's oily water
If your boat sinks you will tell the world

How much you loved everything in it
And if you survive it will be because
You have learned to hate everyone and everything
Growing out of your hopes and your doubts
Your books surely prove it in all of your books
There were the thin ones in Language
And the bad unremembered ones
Prose poems and photobooks
Everything is filled with pronouncements of equanimity
Which you aimed for more often than you attained but
At least you attempted more than the average poem's
    quota
Alongside the contradiction intertextuality disjunction
    and
Cucumber notes
In *Metamorphoses* you invented feeling
As an addition to the process of thought
And it will always remain inside you
In this book in this life on this bed on a boat
The black sea swallowing everything human
You finally realise
Only in writing
Everything that ever needs to be
Saved or discarded—
Including yourself

At this moment in history when

You look out and you find yourself at this moment in
history
You look out and everybody has stopped breathing
And you find yourself dead as we all do
At the hands of someone old rich and white
You know when you were young and you called
yourself a poet
You were a poet and all you had to notice was an
extended metaphor
For the overthrow of the gods and their operatives
You did not realize then that not all writing was a
condensation of sex
You did not realise that it was possible that everything
you loved
Might have to stand up to some kind of a test
You did not realize that men younger than you felt the
need to strike postures
Beside their writing with plastic machine guns and the
desire to impress
And you did not realize that it was desirable to pose
magnificently
From the top of the pile and spit down in order to get
to the top
When you are a poet and you are writing with the
thought
You are part of the solution you are part of the
problem
Laid out on your bed overcome with grief and unloved
because when you were loved

It was never enough and the approval awards and
    support of the angry professors
No longer feeding in to your location at the edge of an
    empire instead of its apex
And your brushing your hair this way and that
Underfunded and morally morbidly obese you now
    realise
The black sea is out there just beyond your door and
    you ask yourself
How important it is to be deluded about the nature of
    mankind
And the nature of art and the necessity of loving
    kindness and interconnection
You would give everything up just to have one final
    breath of your children
And you find it impossible to separate yourself in a city
    filled with lightbulbs
From that particular delusion
They are lighting fires on the outskirts
And they are standing in a line outside food banks
You look out at the buildings and you realize that you
    can see them
Not because of their ability to puncture your eyeballs
    with light
But because you are alive and awake
You look out at everything growing inside the cracks
    that once hosted forests
And you and these ruins
And you notice yourself inside all of those small motions
And they have names but you cannot name them
And you have a purpose but it is not to do something

Every time you were manning the canon
Everything always here in your pencil
All that you have understood and all that you ever
    could one little man
In love with the planet walking over it
Until the world becomes bored or it gets too late
To ignore your realization and the consequence that
You can no longer write
This same old white tale of plunder and delight

You wake up sweating and then

You wake up covered in sweat
Because you find yourself inside a language
Which perhaps you recognize and
Is it a man's language
You never realized that you were or it was
Until you started to pick things up
And go out pointing and feeling
How uncomfortable this all is
On the front of your mouth
Everything here or there which has ever come out
Your pronouncements upon fishing
And upon sound poetry and fish
The works of your enemies in Rome and Berlin and
    London
And your co-dependence therein
All of it accompanied by grimacing and being
    disingenuous
About avoiding disgust
You always felt more comfortable inside
A non-binary language or suburb but how
Do you think you would recognize one if you could see
    one
Approximating itself in the perfect poem
Which you both aspire to and resist
You recognized one once in the formal field of kissing
And you sat down as a result for six months
All that you can do when you are standing up
At the boarding gate
Holding a box of Dunkin' Donuts

Is look for your hand and reach out
For your daughters' thoughts
They you imagine
Understand what you desire
Always a woman's language
Understanding and your chosen genre
Somewhere there is a microphone and you are singing
    into it
Perhaps in a dress and you like the idea of using a
    dictionary
And you shake it
You lose track of your chakras and your eyeball
You shake and you shake in the manner of big plates
And your heart and your art
And your liver and your language
Bang up against every word that you have ever used
You wake up
Sweating and you carry on until you go back
What is this book doing in your hands
If it is standing in for a map
And you are a man
Of sorts and out of sorts
And you are a sea and you are a dictionary
And you contain all the words
Without location small angle or great knowledge
Which you have no alternative but to use
To confirm your great love
In which everything falls
In which everything breaks

When you think about all the people who will possibly read this

Up against a list of all those who you know
Who will not
You are happy as in you are happy that you are sitting
down
So that you do not fall over
And you are happy that you were a writer once
Writing about the world
And you were or are happy that you had some kind of
a voice
In the then dominant language and for some time at
least
You did not feel overwhelmed
By the fact that it came in a sense at the expense of
All the animals and insects
When you were hang-gliding looking down
You would have an intuition about
Every landscape filled from warehouse to palace
With varying degrees of nationalisms
That would make you spill your soup
Walking down the Charing Cross Road
To a gallery or opening
Feeling good to be an artist among the assorted
bohemians
Noticing but not knowing what to do about your role in
its manufacture
You were an artist with the ability to take a plane out
of it
And flying over forests and factories you remember

Working in a factory frying
Pigs for pork scratchings for a fortnight
And you worked for three weekends in a field picking
    beans
Converting your labour into albums by Can and Kate
    Bush
And you did not really really work
In a factory slitting the scrotums of animals and pulling
    stuff out
Or rimming their skins holding boxes breathing in car
    parts
Bending forward over a floor sorting grain grinding
Until you induce curvature of the spine
But others did
You look down at the holes and the oceans
And you think of these things now
Here they are in your poem and here you are too
    sadly
Interdependent at the edge of the continent under a
    bed
In a notebook or boat dreaming of either returning to
    the capitol
Or overcoming it somehow
If your imagination worked differently
And you could successfully practise non-attachment
Instead of just reading the books
If your imagination and your letters could burn out
If they could burn out
All that you have learned about being human
Ways how to read faster or less
If only you could go back to a time

Before you had seen anything that could hurt you
Meaning anything arranged in time and space
The only time you get out of it
Is when you think about who will possibly read this
Speaking aloud before strangers
A kind of apparently prosaic consciously artificial
Consciously virtually fictional writing
Which nonetheless is an acutely painful distant echo
Of the paralyzed poetic in which verse is allowed to
    erupt
Occasionally at certain points of irony or pressure
But never enough to assert its autonomy
As a fluency of lines
Giving way to feeling
Feeling suddenly
You know—very ____
Very ____

You write it down and there it is

When you are writing a poem
And you are thinking there is nothing
When you are writing a poem
There is not the same potential for variation
You write it down and there it is that's the version
Or else you delete that version and replace it with
    another
It's almost like erasing the knowledge that appears
Rather than representing it because the knowledge
Properly understood consists in the future potential
    variability
Of the detail and the whole narration
Film copy clouds the landscape
The moment thinking stops and you are left with
    repetition
Beginning and ending with questions concerning the
    whole narrative
What makes you think then that knowledge appears
As opposed to ignorance
Or perhaps error is just as much knowledge
When you are writing a poem by Ovid
Making use of the face to indicate heightened states
With electronic props to see into the future
There is not the same potential for variation
When you are writing a poem beside the black sea
On the edge of an invisible empire with goozleum
    glasses
Your magical power is a language-based approach to
    culture

Race and gender conflated or contrasting periods
With no central character combined with that of
    invisibility
And this is what the poem as an achieved object
    directly abolishes
Masters a master plan the master discourse and the
    master race
There is nothing more beautiful than this and
There is nothing more beautiful than there are more
    beautiful things than Beyoncé
You write it down and there it is

It gets to the point that you read things you cannot repeat

It gets to the point that you read things
You cannot repeat about love not because
You have forgotten but because you remember
There is nothing else in your head left to think about
   which you don't want
And you don't want the point in the book where it says
You are a man because you think
You have no place in the new world
Because of all that you did in the old
And you are both angry and confused
But you have already said that
The world is filled with so much content that most of it
Spills over the sides and you go out and teach that
The world is improved when you say that
The world has form you asshole
But it does not
Think about the combative nature of all discourse
And you wonder what right you have to be a statistic
Upon social media broadcasting your minority or
   diminishing tastes
You prefer the word spirits when thinking of humans
When you think about the development of the
   seven-blade razor
And the tampon tax
Patti Smith said Rimbaud said something on cassette
About the future belonging to women
Every time you look in the paper
You wanted your love to approximate song
And you wanted your poetry to touch everyone

But that was wrong
All the time
You spend your days writing
Watch your daughters
Grow older
And puke in a book

For the second noble truth of the Buddha the Buddha

Shakyamuni Gautama spoke
The second noble truth
Out of four
The line runs something something
About suffering and attachment
Suffering coming due to life in its nature being
Unsatisfactory or imperfect
Like a house at an angle or cracked and when
You think about your writing
And all the places
You read it
And were happiest—
In a snowstorm with Michael Gizzi
In Gulf of Maine Books
To three humans
Two dogs
And the vanishing light

For Michael

Nobody with a tie gives a fuck

You have to face facts at some point in your life
In the seas of South London
You think about who you could ask for forgiveness and
  you make a list
And you start crossing names off
Because the hero of the problem of the content
  material and form
Cannot determine the difference between life and art
Your poems of crossing allowed you to leave something
  and become something other
In your more conceptual pieces it is helpful and more
  dangerous
Having had knowledge to discard it
In your moments of doubt it is impossible to make love
  and not produce knowledge
Oh which is a revolutionary action
Being bored or being boring before the invention of
  neon
You are doing something for the futures of all men and
  women
There is cold brew coffee to keep you awake
You loved the dictionary and making things up and
You loved coming back to the city after Christmas in the
  country
And an end to white faces
And you loved entering squats and housing co-ops
You loved making badges and going on protests
And you thought the world could always be good if
  only

You could be good and refract social progress
You thought about the benefits of psychosomatic drugs
There were things in your life which up till that point in
    the history of humankind
Could never exist
Giraffes and anglerfish haptic writing and cameras
The world changes when you ejaculate you once wrote
As a carrier of an ideological position and not as a
    mere formal resource
You go down in parks because you are supposed to
The natural world is before you and all the good
    people
In hospitals who used to do good dying no wonder
There are people on the streets sleeping under
    newspapers
We believed that it was okay to go to our beds and
That it was okay to dream of new music
But all over the world a part of it is dark growing
    darker
And inside it there is a secret secret service
Which never sleeps

In the painting by Turner titled Ovid Banished From Rome

You can almost make out at the author point
Where the Romantic and the Classical meet
It is the point where being or becoming human has
    become impossible
And all corners of the empire the structures and statues
    and columns
Piled up in the light falling to approximate banks
There in the painting if this is the model
Surrounded by property speculators in the painting of
    the west
The author leans a little into the picture
And the trash in the foreground before him
Boxes and pizzas handles food containers
Other characters in the photographs of exile have
    been noted
An enormous arm on a barge or three people in a
    field
A dog of sorts and a black and white watch
In the painting by Turner the character may be
Bakhtin or Mandelstam or yourself
And the pose may be reckless or wretched the way
    colours contain feeling
Coming up out of the human soup
Sooner or later the filter of history will inevitably
    sweep the filth from my head
Bukharin said just as thinking gets sloppy over time
The trajectory of the artist is towards the academy and
    you stink

Of your desire to become recognized in this letter no
    less
Occupying a high point in the audited landscape
In the painting by Delacroix you are reclining
In the painting by Delacroix and just
As in Turner your life is a mess
When something does not end in both paintings
There are some undefined characters huddled together
In the bottom right corner you are too sick to see them
But of course you cannot see either painting
How Delacroix has located you and his mountains
Lying down and how for so you imagine
It is a white patch in a round dish
You pause to win the love of women
The sunset over four evenly distributed band lots
In which you held my hand
You know that is the mystery of painting
And the mystery of love and the mystery of living
Waking beside the black sea the container vessels
And the innumerable bodies
If you pick up this mystery and you look at it closely
You wonder what will happen in your poem
Sadness
If you decide to discard it or
Claim you've found the solution

***In Hesiod's Theogony there is an ancient debate
concerning the meaning of the word chaos***

In Hesiod's Theogony the cosmic region represented
    thereby
Cannot be either the earth or the sky but is the gap
    between these
Baudelaire went there but turned his back on it
Returning to narcissism and the consolations of sex
In this cosmic region everything and in this cosmic band
You have located your character and your character
Disrupts the narrative event floating in the zone
    between the real world
And the one that you imagined the world to have
You cannot see it because you distrust the law
In this orientalist fantasy
You doubt the power of your mind to make things
    happen
And can smell the smell of King Zog to the north
With his pocket lighters and Hungarian shot
In your world you know that civilization depends upon
    writing
Your sex books brought you nothing but trouble
In the cosmic region Baudelaire's chair and you elude
    the banality of the received idea
Bought at airports in books about alien visitations and
    the Kray Twins
They come looking for insights and you find them their
    verbs and their relations how
Can you be sure that you miss other humans when you
    doubt that they happen

You order them to do things and they do because of
    your language
There is a separate place for food made out of paper
    and for food made from blood
There is a woman and there is a daughter in the capitol
    representing human relations
And they do or do not exist if you cannot feel them in
    time you do not
Care because the sea has sucked of your language
    and you are
Hovering above the stage the sea is a table
The stars are the names for points of light and they
    make you
And you and they and we in this cosmic region
I do not think of it all of the time
When your foot in the morning falls upon what was
    once your beloved's comb
The destruction of western values fills your leg
It wants to know what happens after everything in the
    world has happened
You are a person from the future reading this
And the things that you know about it are different
Like pencil stubs and big dumb birds
You have taken a space under my bed
And you are warm and light in this cosmic region
There is the author and there is the empire
And there is the beloved and there is intertextuality
But it is concerned with single texts as opposed to a
    dialectic
In your socialism
Blaise Cendrars appears

With a message from the king of the gypsies
Here he is
With a line about potatoes and what he says was once
His secret weapon
Not giving a fuck
Your character becomes indistinct
In the face of the canon
The war is not over and his hand is still lost

***You are one of the modern lovers it says here and you
discover yourself then***

One of the postmodern ones having left the prior
conditions behind
Asleep in a new country where there is no sun or you
cannot find it
Your exile is so internal that the world barely notices
every time you eat soup
You pretend that you do not get out from under the
bed
But such a thought is impossible to leave in a city
without grass leaves or green beans
What else is impossible
When you were buying records and all you did was
listen
Nobody knew the goal you were pursuing
Perhaps it was something free from language
Because you had had enough of it or you did not know
your self
Sometimes just the smell of something human would turn
you on
To the narrow space of the Tao in which underlying
behaviours go unnoticed
If you place your forehead upon the water when it is
flat
You imagine that you can go back to Rome and you
can hear it
You think of your daughters and you think of their
daughters

When you held them around the resurgence of tender
    feelings
With respect to the world now it would be good to be
    shot of everything
Your inner ear is a shambles whose desire is to have
    someone to love
And the power to repatriate the world through
    tenderness
When news comes of the presidential summit
You disappear into longing for a different return
With no specific place in mind without a positive
    fantasy
This is a condition where there is no longer any
    familiarity
You were one of the modern lovers
Flying with your poems towards a platform leaning into
    a mic tapping it then speaking
How much you love potato salad the moment you first
    kiss
The language fills something for you to abandon it
Would cause you to come but you cannot if
You want to extract the beloved body from its historical
    circumstance
And stay safe in the same way it is unimportant to
    understand
The instructions on a bottle of sunblock
In order to get rid of the self and its attendant
    suffering in exile
The first thing you have to do is construct an other face
    down

In the Black Sea one way of making yourself foreign to
   the world is
To become indifferent to public opinion
To become invisible and to embrace failure still
When you close your eyes
However hard you try—you always find
Your face wet when it wakes

Everyone's story ends in terror

Marina Tsvetaeva for one moment repeatedly after
    another
Refusing the imperative to inform on themselves
You know that you are impossibly free
When you've been buried all that you have left is the
    library
And your children's old bones
Handing you whatever it is that you want me to do
You can hear the sound of poppers and rappers
    reading
And you can wrap your legs around beautiful
Eggs you saying something profound about something
    on Venus
It snows metal and rains sulphuric acid Babe
We are doomed to repeat the mistakes of our books
Due to genetic defects
Reading this Latin primer
As a book of instructions
You must repeat
I will have done things when
You want to use I
Love instead of he or she loves you use am
O instead of am at
Because everything is hidden in the ending
It says that a woman gives
Money to a girl the girl hides the money with a rod
A farmer is ploughing the land and kicks the girl's money
He gazes at the money and dances
O land I love money

The girl beats the farmer and the farmer attempts flight
Why is he avoiding the girl
Because the girl is beating the farmer with a rod
Why is she beating the farmer with a rod
Because he praises the money and attempts flight
In Latin you only need the separate word *I*
When you wish to be very emphatic
Imagine a countryside far away from anywhere
With no fridge with no lights
This is the land out of which
I must write

When atoms are travelling down through empty space

And when atoms are travelling down through empty
    space
By their own weight at quite indeterminate times and
    places
There is the possibility that they will be
Shot by racists and lost
If not for this swerve everything would fall down
Like raindrops through the abyss of space
Going to live in the possibilities offered by the giving
    of a meditation
Teaching or poetic reading after all
You were the first avant-garde poet in the history of
    the world to be kettled
And you can prove it in verse
If anyone supposes that the heavier atoms on a straight
    course
Through empty space exist in the epic and could
    outstrip the lighter ones
And fall on them from above
Thus causing impacts that might give rise to generative
    motions
Stand-up routines in nightclubs
    revolution-through-humor
As practiced in Yugoslavia or dissolution of ego
They are wrong
You are under a bed and the bombs are no longer
    falling
And you are under a bed because you know that the
Times when they stop is always and only a lull

If you close your eyes you can feel the atoms swerving
But not to avoid the colour of your skin
And you can ask yourself if all movement is connected
One day you are making love on a lawn and then the
    next
Swerving from your own course at no set time or place
Distracted by flyovers and freeways heading west
There is a cloud in Minecraft the way that you built it
And you occasionally go there to relax
Your t-shirt says that you believe in unconditional love
    at poetry readings
And your shirt is covered with flowers but you wore that
    one out
It was good to be alive before the empire grew tired
And it was good to have known love before the
    invention of disco or internet
You really thought that women and men would be
    equal before the end of 1977
But you did not reckon on men
There is a picture of a skinny white girl on the side of a
    building
In every city and in every city there is a rich or poor
    white girl
Spitting on somebody else
And there will always be somebody else praying
To somebody else
And their heads will be touching and all the gods and
    the cars and their stuff
And these atoms not visible and the injustices and the
    possibility that they will be
Shot by racists

They are choosing the paint for the walls of their
bedroom
And they are thinking and kissing
You see them wherever you go but you do not really
see them
When you close your eyes under the bed
During a break in the bombing
You can hear them breathing and you can hear them
coming
You know they will never stop coming
For you
There is a list

Because you are an artist and you are entitled

And because you are an artist
Who has leveraged their privilege
In front of other artists upon panels
In order to obtain funding
You are in a film with Queen Latifah you think
This has something to do with being in an underground
    cell
In Eastern Europe and that you are both sleepers
Perhaps there will come a time when you receive a call
You wonder how it will come and you wonder if Latifah
    really is a queen
How she is managing in hiding if she is and
How you will find her from your position in a film in the
    future
From your position at your desk or your bed
And while you are in hiding
In an art film
Everything is structured around this anticipation of
    finding another beloved
Noting that the one with a capital is constructed to be
    a punishment
In this city in which you struggle
In this city you cannot even buy shoelaces from men
    with beards
It is about 410 degrees below zero
There is no cheese and no pancake
Perhaps you are an actor in Back To The Future
There are no books by your desk where there once
    were books

Everything real is imagined first
In order to be imagined you like Marina Tsvetaeva
Lack the impassivity that is so invaluable for an
    investigator
At the demo you carry a placard
Over which your passive-aggressive petitioning merely
    hovers
You are walking down the Travessera de Gracia in
    Barcelona
And you are walking down Market Street in San
    Francisco
Towards city hall
You are so tiny lyrical and anonymous
That you cannot get arrested
How did you get here and how did anybody get
    anywhere
At this point in the film
It is time being European to insert a sex scene
It is time to stop and it is time to give up
And it is time to lie down and they call for your more
    buff body double
Love—you have finally realized—at fifty-years-old
Everybody looks lost

***When you are less angry the landscape recedes to a
horizon or a moment that clangs***

In the soundscape of the Danube there are
Those who make me want to puke over my shoulder
when no news comes
You loved Tishe Amijo Head when she left your body in
Oxnard and all that remained
Was a postcard of the beats
A book bearing your name may or may not exist
Moulding a jello map from prominent bumps
That book may contain invectives against the
government
Along with portions of August and forgotten poets
I take hold of the toe of infinite power and loved Tishe
Amijo Head
She lived in a car with a bank robber called Buck when
we made love
The book you may have written you believe makes no
mention of this
When a woman leaves her body they leave yours also
To listen to the Danube but no longer see it
When you lie flat beneath the wine dark sea and feel
the fresh water touching it
There are marks on your arms where the secret police
promised to twist them
Turning away from metonymy towards the space that
the globe opens up
Things you wish you had never written
Thinking you had hidden them in the lungs and the liver
And the spaces between letters

When you are less happy you try everything
    revolutionary
To turn the clock back to a time before
Jesus you think
You do not know if there was ever a time when the
    secret police
Did not know where you lived
When you are busy initiating and documenting a more
    sexual mode
It is harder to tell if any of the participants work for
    the filth in Latin
To fight with a person you must use *cum*
But not for the weapon
For example *I fight the monkey with a rose*
Cum simia rosa pugno
In England *thou* is commonly used
Because in that country they have no need for police
Everyone who lives there is dead or asleep

For Tishe Amijo Head

It always feels like the end of history

At the end of history at the end of the world at the end
    of your life
At the start of the summer or the middle of spring
When you look out and remember
Your dreams of every naked or partially dressed
    floating thing
And it always feels like the end when you open the
    paper packed with bodies
And everything is too black or too white or too fat or
    too thin
First they bring back the emperor and then when your
    powers are failing
There is the body mass index and the metric to assess
    impact
When you look through the fence into the detention
    centre
You do not know what you can achieve
Because it is late and or your eyesight is failing
But you can hear people weeping
You thought you could see the future but it did not
    include grabbing women
That ending one way of believing and another of
    being
You thought that if you wrote well it would change
    everything in reality
A blood orange granissat on the Ronda Sant Antoni in
    Barcelona in 2001
Had greater effect and was more convincing

In all corners all humans wrapping or unwrapping
    plastic-wrapped fingers
Laid out in trays carried inside boxes in bigger boxes
    in bigger boxes eating and excreting
You realise poetry is positive
Not because it does something but because it does
    nothing and includes everything
You can remember solid hollows and you can
    remember bits of things
Perhaps this is the real curse of being human
The deep red juice of the orange combining with the
    ice for one moment
When a human falls in love with a human
On a boat for example or in a queue or in a
    landscape
Package or bank holiday levee or level crossing
The world changes all of your life you were feeling too
    much of everything
Because you were feeling too much of someone
Typing poems in the night on a phone with your finger
Every time a man grabs a woman
With a heart full of something
More than a poem grabs a woman when a man grabs
    a woman
With more force than a poem to which
Noone knows or listens
Who can live with these facts

You go days without seeing your daughter sooner or later

You go years without seeing anything
You find yourself standing alone most of the time in
    passenger channels
Connecting free trade regions distributing your
    privilege freely
In search of the beloved
Occasionally you get news through your papers about
    bees dying
You are
Thinking about one landing on her hand
When she was in a bed in the summer asleep
You were
With me for a while I believed that
Two humans could reduce their loneliness to a point
That they could put it on a mantelpiece or could make
    it an island or
Something grand away from which to sail and feel
    safe
You have some photos in black-and-white the sea
    being
Black and the sky being white the lower half of the
    thing shaped like a father
Beneath the other action always imagined
Always escaping sky you have
Li Po reading in a silent night he says
Moonlight before my bed perhaps frost on the ground
I lift my head and see the moon lower my head
Pine for home the cup sound a cup makes
In a city that is subject to drone strikes

You get under your bed with a book
And it is good that it is the one in your head
Because due to blackouts brownouts and occasional
    attacks
You have something about anarchism in Barcelona and
    you emptied it out
Long ago in attending to the dictates of love
When you did not live in a war zone food thoughts
Without sight of good and your bread demands for
    equality
The supreme court is stacked with vampires
You cannot reach your daughter
You wake find yourself alive and
The Black Sea comes up somewhat in the space
Talking to yourself upon a street at midnight
When the bombs stop
And the weather has taken all the sounds out of your
    mouth
And you are an artist and you are a coward
At those moments
You do not know which is worse

Nothing is easy and nothing works anymore

Concerning your desire to become a woman you do not
    touch
Anything with your voice
You cannot continue to breathe easily because long
    ago
You realized your anatomy could no longer be right
In the way that you approach death
How much I miss your hand on my pills and your neck
You no longer look like anything nor be determined by
    eros
Which was the country you grew up in
A boy by a lake
And from it you could hear trains on their way to North
    Bay plunge into snow and take on most of its
    character
You would dream of the beloved and their beautiful
    cheques
You would call in the morning for them to come on top
    of you
Until you could no longer breathe
Everything you ever said about love was no good
You are recently deceased and you are all pronouns
Somebody is taking your words down in an imaginary
    letter
In an imaginary letter
You want La Bamba to be played at your funeral
In the true path of the ninja
You cannot transform your shape
But you can darken your face

There is great joy in the mountains when the news comes

And there is great joy on the plains
In the satellite towns reaching out
Through the wires in untidy buildings
Occupied by the speakers of different languages
Clad in inflammable packaging
News comes that the president has been exploded or
    shot
Although not strictly true we believe it
Not the logical sequence and abstract hierarchy of
    ideas
But the composition which ordains the succession of
    forms
Images tones rhythms and sonorities
We go over and place biting ants on his body
We pray for peace we hope that they will start on his
    face
We pray for peace we look at his parts
And cannot help but notice the flow of toxins
Between the armpit and the neck
There is a screen around the back and the blue light
    coming off
It is possible during moments of maximum compassion
To escape the shared relationship between abuser and
    abused
Commerce and the individual past and its opposing
    banality
You realize during sitting practice or during moments in
    banks
That you are not something

Useful and you realize that your body takes up space
How much you exist due to hate
Being by a bed by a sea by a lake
Watching bodies repeatedly wash up
Beasts lacerated by plastic human sorts as you imagine
    them
Swimming with their babies plunging their noses into
    the mud
To earn a living
I am writing inside you even though I am outside
Everything important in life
On the edge of everything slipping I think
I think of kissing you in 24 volumes and the decline and
    fall of the Roman Empire
I think of you always
Living between a mountain and a new genre
The touch of your moustache
My beautiful wife
Almost coming at the sight

Because you are a confused human being and fading without coffee

You write all you can before you are dead
To make sense of it
Books are the best
Piled up against the windows and doors
They go on when you don't
Used damaged then abandoned everything in the
    world
You had a hand in that somebody
Loved the same but different
How many times have you wanted to die
Or for you to
To make one of us happy
It would be exciting to perish in a plane crash
Instead of cancer you died once
In a review by Steve Evans and once when you were a
    father
In the Somers Town
You never quite left
This is your third epitaph poem and they are getting
    easy to write
Preoccupied with someone coming in
And your being
Stamped on and anonymous
In your lifetime in every tier of government
Your body lacks a plot
50% of the world's animals have already gone
The small bones in your head all say no to Bob Dylan

And there is no such thing as a functioning author
    function
Only the heart somewhere and always
Because they have sold everything
Hovers above the Black Sea
Black itself because abandoned
And black itself before attaining experimental form
Who wants love when they could have had success
It is easy to die when your children get lost
This is your third epitaph poem and it is your second
    best
Words piled up in the shape of a person
Via some kind of breakage
You long to resist

If autobiographical fiction is a map of the self

And you find yourself misrepresented upon that map
Then you think I did come too quickly in a house in
    Osaka
The appeal located in pleasure domes
Protection from 100% humidity and protesting
    complete ignorance
When you love at least the idea of loving everything
    on a map
Which starts with the cloud of unknowing
Your original face or some literary movement based
    upon testing your voice
Here in exile upon the topography of excluded culture
    and exploitation
There are wooden structures which you could live in
Ones of stone and others of felt
And there are gated communities located beside the
Red and the Black and the White and the Yellow Seas
Constructed by venture capitalists
Cockroaches eating the possibilities of being human in
    billions of homes
Most of the time you click to indicate your absence
In any meaningful discourse
There is a film starring Claudia Cardinale
And you see her as the answer to your problems with
    genre fiction
You remind yourself that you need to be an I
If you want to win prizes awards or attract serious
    funding
In your latest publication

A group of musical clowns transforms your bedroom or
   space
Ship space into a circus in which the actors perform
   your life for five minutes
You have crossed whole seas constellations apart
And you have lost them in hospitals
Looking at the map of superficial emotions without
   coffee
You are way to the left
The Black Sea is full of pinholes
Every one of which
Indicates an anonymous body
Just for one moment you think
Of Ornette Coleman meeting Don Cherry for the first
   time
And for the last time
In your life perhaps
You need nothing else

And so when you have left your apartment and you have left it

First of all you close the doors and windows of your
  apartment
And you walk through the Zona Industrial on the
  outskirts
To the west the OMV gas station Power Station
Gara Oil Terminal and Carrefour
And then across the railroad tracks and
You are somewhere in the night beside cranes
A kiosk which reads Gelaterie Italia although it is not
And you are beside or outside or inside a black stretch
  of water
You do not know this much and you maybe still play the
  banjo
When you play anything after a fashion
When you play anything and your voice somewhere
Between bad alto or tenor with irregular rhythm
Your songs think of something and they leave you
Maybe they leave you if they have a place to escape
Because songs by the sea or in the mountains
You are a thing good at registering
The day is the day and the night is the night
You are an I and you do not like its shape
Your daughter was somewhere in Africa
When you were arrested so even then when you love
  everyone
It is impossible to be someone
With a banjo on your knee
If are thinking about your feet

Even though you cannot see them
And you are thinking about your arms and your heart
Even though you do not feel them
You are standing between a lifetime of bad decisions
And the moment you stop breathing
The council of the city of Rome will revoke your exile
In December 2017
The last time you held another person it was
Two thousand and ten years ago
The last time you held another person
It was A.D. 8 they were 1709.5 kilometers away to the
    west
You can never go back

Everyone smashes it at the office party and

Everyone smashes it at the office party because
Humans love to fuck but don't film it with your phone in
    case
You kiss a fascist or press up against one
It is inadvisable to get drunk with frustration or anger
    you see
The rich getting and they go around everywhere in
    helicopters and jets
At weekends to festivals and private shit
As long as no filming is involved it's important to smash
    it to get on
At Cambridge or Oxford Harvard or the Sorbonne
    such behaviour brings prizes
In Rome when you smash it away from the friendlier
    black shirts
You never know who's coming on they say
The difference between a communist and a fascist is
    twenty years and
Who's counting your solipsism in an aesthetically
    self-conscious performance
Calling for a total overhaul of the social functions of
    poetry objects
Buildings and places the things that persist amid
    anarchy
I smashed it at the office party twice and invented the
    elegy as lament
If you are a poet and you would rather not fight but
Fuck is it acceptable to misrepresent yourself in front of
    the police

And is it understandable if you crawl up the ass of the
    authorities
To get what you want while flipping them the finger
    back
Is that some kind of transpersonal integrity
The world is complicated after you have filmed it and
    posted on facebook
And it is cruel if you are called out about your
    imaginary illnesses to get attention
Or deny being somebody's girl at the party
This contrast of past and present applies not just to
    your exile
But also to the enemies of imperialism an empire of
    memory
And a realm of language rooted in the rhetoric of
    visuality
Screwing wildly with meaning
Smashing it at the literary soiree
Conjured up in a futuristic history
Announced through an unstable tense system

You steal a canister of laughing gas

And then you steal another canister of laughing gas
And that's just the start
I got MRSA in my left ball
And I read everything
I was a frequenter of dancehalls
And I was a small thing leaning on walls
In the Hammersmith Palais
Listening to Billy Boyo sing
One spliff a day keeps the evil away
Till they call the tanks in

Everything's living and everything's feeling

Everyone who does not get what they want and
    nobody gets it
But what do they do with theories and documents of
    contemporary art
You make things from places where you have taken
    impressions
And arrange them to make you feel good
If the purpose of being human is to consume things and
    to be cosmologically wrong
It was good to be famous up to a point
And it was good to be considered a particular type of
    transformation
And to make things again you do not make love to
    something you make love with
One piece about no new ideas entering this work
Because you never put your hand on my neck I imagine
    I go there now
To change art and destroy ego you can do that if you
    have a camera
And you do not have an audience
In the history of world
And all music I regret any discomfort my presence is
    causing you just as I am sure you regret
The discomfort your racism is causing me
In the eyes of everyone I leave there now still with some
    small flowers and the project of
Hope for inexhaustible rejoicing
You follow that statement with a white plate piled with
    green peppers and some salt I imagine

Your hand on my neck
I was full of the matrix of events in history in order to
   eroticize time you were
In the shower between truth and fiction in everyday life
Everybody is dead who does not give you what you
   want
You are an artist and the purpose of writing is to reach
And you reach and you reach
The ultimate word of the world and about the world
   has not yet been spoken
The sea is too black to swim out of
And you are too dark to stand out

Then likewise actually even

You write yet another memorial defamatory pamphlet
   full of zeal
From your favoured position from beneath the black
   water
Asking for someone ahead or sent forward to
   remember you
With love or to grant you a pardon
In addition and out of helplessness you send with it
Your final magic formula being a curse or a hex not
   worth mentioning
Having allowed sadness to wash out the magic poetry
You read once correctly shaped and consistent the
   knowledge
You will never again eat a sandwich or look at a cat
   thought
And you deathly in banality thinking of
Everything as my writing if you thought it
Concerning your appetite for intercourse in the Jardins
   de Luxembourg
When you write the word *etoiles*
You don't mean the things in the sky but the words in
   the book and
They look back at you
Long tedious boundless far off and of specific length
One truth being everyone dies wanting something it
   seems
On the human plane one gains a tolerance for
   destruction

Your A.C.A.B. tattoo proves that you can put up with
    pretty much anything
In order to avoid motion
Everybody turns to god when the world loses interest
Air looks good in its arrangement around your desk
    space
Gail Johnson's grandmother died at 90
Wishing she'd had lots more cock we breathed in her
    smoke
It was a lifetime of fags sadness
In the English sense and things lost in the body
Large intense tedious and assiduous
If you look closely enough every human is beautiful
But no-one is looking
I see this as the beauty of your protest

For Sean Bonney

Because to write is to give aesthetic value

And because to write is to judge the world according
    to the senses
We are not Ovid
Informed by a voracious study of various scientific and
    metaphysical systems
I am the thing itself interested in any era you know
    what to do with John Keats
Because everyone does
You open your mouth in the process of poetry only later
Will human beings be freed from this process
I sit in my one-room apartment and write for three
    months
In which the elegist can place diffuse intangible
    feelings of grief
And thereby win release from suffering
Or so I thought
And then there is murder and the gospel sound
There is life in the provinces and good air when you
    climb to the highest point
Gazing over the topography of racism and despair
In the metropolis at least there were 24 hour opening
    food outlets
Avant-garde towers swinging at the top of Brick Lane
Broken trains boarded up bookstores and Jamaicans
Jeff you could smell the money and taste the piss
You could be a man or a woman or a chicken and no
    one would notice
You publish and perish give up repeatedly and give up
    giving up

Giving up your organs recycling batteries and giving
up thought
One hundred years from now they will be flying in
beans from Venus
Just because you know something about everything or
everything about something
Doesn't mean that you know how to knit the beloved
As you come back into being from your trip
This time you will never do it again
You may have no use for the bastards who run the
western empire
But you have to confess
They need you much less

Everyone you love disappoints you because

Everyone you love disappoints you because they are
    gone
Because of the river and the frozen summer
Everything pointless and because you need nothing
    beyond eating it
There are hundreds of reasons no-one visits your hovel
Everything is in your mind
You make lists of political activists
Sent to the gulags poets in the foothills of mountains
Mystics or resisters sent to Kazakhstan
If you had won the Forward Prize for Poetry
The secret police would never have found you
It was like looking through a milky glass sheet
And you do not like to be beside the seaside
    remembering your feelings
Everyone you love has been crushed by the empire
And everyone you love believes that their needs are
    more important
Than collective action and they hand you their
    chapbooks
You were the poet who wrote of your enemies and your
    allegiances and
Your insecurities and your doubts and you were an
    attempt at truth
But you were too much of a dick
You were an autobiography made out of bullshit
And you had far too much front
The final goal being the overthrow of self by inflating
    before popping the self

Inside one method you just keep getting slapped and
    wake up
On the eleventh of August in Koktebel at twelve noon
When the sun is at its very zenith
That is at the very top of the head
At the hour when the shadow has conquered the body
And the body is dissolved in the body of the world
At his favourite hour of nature for the 11th of August is
    clearly
The noon of the year at twelve o clock
The poet Maximilian Voloshin died
It is not the same year that Marina Tsvetaeva took her
    life
And it is not the same thing as the death of the author
Being the most beautiful theory in the recent struggle
Her book is a best seller and she is growing notorious
    and famous in equal measure
You are a little in love with her
Verbs and her position
In your understanding of how to unravel the puzzle
You take your sincerity to an agent but refuse to
    surrender the film rights
And in spite of your emails and petitions
Love-notes impeccable dental hygiene and knowledge
    of high-brow novels
You are too something to be of use
Except as an exemplar of the reason for the fight
Against entitlement and power and then
You must learn not how to avoid capture
But how not to surrender
Everyone you love leaves for CAConrad

According to Nazim Hikmet
Your struggle is this

No-one wants to die in Kingston-on-Thames

Kingston Ontario or Kingston Jamaica
No kings needed anywhere
All people everywhere breathing in
Heavy metal under heavy manners
Every hour is just another hour among the gone
Despots and rolling river
Besides which clearly
Everybody dies here or everywhere
Because money rules
Not you
In the black velvet of Soviet night
Petrograd is transparent on the tongue
Like berries are and the next poem
Is for Marina Tsvetaeva
In the sense that one can see death everywhere
You go
You long to hug your big friends
Osip Marina Trotsky
Tu Fu Boethius Ovid Bakhtin
Everywhere everyone
Fly away home
Your house is on fire
Your children are gone

You grew bored of being loved when you were loved

And now that you want to be loved
Your ideas and your shape have grown invisible and
impossible
So you climb to the highest point in the city and from
there
The warehouses and wharves obscured by old lovers
and poets
You were one of them once but nowadays
Horns come in to port carrying pirates
In the gospel on poetic imagination and reverie
The Golden Harps record two singles now lost
You steal a line and mix it with some pharmaceutical
instructions
In the hope that your brain or your body or your soul
will be able to relinquish control
Of the lower regions of the Danube the golden age of
paraphernalia
Spiritual materialism and the deteriorating aqueous
humor inside your left eyeball
In the morning reaching out to read something
The words bang beneath the lids
Will you ever become reconciled to being banished
from Europe you wonder
How it is possible to drown in a boat and
How it is possible to stop yourself drowning by getting
shot
In the poem with full stops
The poem offers no answers if that makes it a good
one

You flick your head to swoosh back the clutter that
   gathers around the goldfish and junk
If the job of the poem or the job of the poet is to
   create a clear space
In which past and present are resisted and all being
   comes to focus
This or any particular instant
You take out your work which is not working
You put your left hand on the formica-topped table
To avoid scorching and with your right out of sight you
   look out of the window
And you reach for a knife

Reading is best if you start out weak and

Reading is best if you start out fragile aroused or
    intense
Picking future time from the text in a position of
    decayed utterance
In *The Pillow Book of Sei Shonagon*
You encounter yourself in a number of positions
With magnificent hair and a toothache
In the Buildings of England your cast iron columns
And extraordinary foliage capitals
Doing this because it is romantic to leave the body
In a state of boredom or excitement
The way it would be good to walk away from words
Their deracinating physical and psychological effects
And probably posthumous responses to maladjustment
Reading does not force you to choose a country
In order to be considered rational or balanced
The exilic experience in your book is a failure by
    nature
So they took away everything
You are high above Berlin in an ill-fitting jacket
In the film *Wings of Desire*
A neo-marxist angelic substance pontificating
On the corrupting influence of capitalism
And the evils of popular culture that placated its
    masses
The only home truly available in exile though fragile
    and vulnerable
Is in writing or dialogue
All over the world there are naked men and women

But none of them are yours
Where you come from
There are bombs going off and a longing for war
Thinking of our bodies and the poems we once loved
Home is a place under the bed
Your voice just one voice with its yearning for discourse
Instead of two worlds you have none
The house is past
The whole of your life up to now has been one of
  unconscious exile
And a lack of endurance
You are nothing compared to cool jazz or custard
And are happy to swim in it till the clocks all go back
Then when you look up
The whole landscape
Is flat fascist black

You would give it all up if you could escape from this place and

You would give it all up if you could have one last
   good fuck
Either classically inflected or with the whiff of the
   carnivalesque
Feeling neither Baudelaire nor bonny beside the Black
   Sea
But you have found yourself on a cushion in the zen hall
And you have found yourself in the library
And you have found yourself perhaps a little drunk
Wanting to escape from something you see in yourself
   like H.P. Lovecraft
Horizontal on a pad or yoga mat
It dawning upon you that there is nothing that you have
   left that is worth giving up
Although it is good being a poet because
Even when you are patchy unconsciously macho or
   mediocre
You can sit down and you can think you are a genius /
   unnoticed
It is good to think poet-thoughts about clouds seas and
   trees
Until some romantic other comes along and defaces
   them
Poetry is stronger than love perhaps if you subscribe to
   the small press aesthetic
Your body is good and then it is not
How strange it is to notice age spots on your hands
Beauty around the eyes of Joanne Kyger

You for one wanting to be hot at the front and cool at
    the back
You imagine that you would still do things in private
And it's right in a way to be doing them
Alone with a ukulele
And it's wrong in a way to believe that the world owes
    you a living
But the world owes almost everyone a living at first
All people building to a peak at least
Until they fuck it all up

Sometimes you cannot help the person you love and sometimes

You were falling off a wall and would say something
   made up from a book
Sometimes you think about the things they did to the
   Jews often
And the things they did to the gays and the things they
   did to the disabled
And the things they did to the gypsies
The fresh water freezing over the heavier salt the way
   that the Danube never stops coming
Having learned to be fearful of Vikings
Once you liked closing your eyes and not knowing
   whose were the hands and whose were the fingers
You ask yourself what Sun Ra would do if he were in
   this situation and you conclude that
He would demand the elimination of all karmic
   obstruction
There is a naked man in the opposite block learning to
   play the violin
In the stories we tell each other
After the invention of electricity
And the invention of semaphore
Standing by a headwater river or lake you wanted to
   feel loved for a change more than ever
You felt love
Going to the Hanshin Tigers game
You do not know if that happened
Hoping to see everything with the soft warm place
   between your legs

All the gypsy bands you ever heard stick out their
     trumpets
As if night had her cradle there
Sleep
Remembered or imaginary
And the invention of honey

For Thomas Evans

You are doomed anyway and you are doomed if you believe in gods

If you believe in gods because it proves you are dumb
and then if you don't
You are in trouble because you are exactly the type
who the gods love to fuck
Being moderate in discourse and argument holding
yourself and others to account for failures in logic
It is hard being a rational human by the side of
something appalling
However hard you want to slap it to revert to type
There is a visualization which involves forests and there
is a book which occasionally works
If you could be anything you would dissolve into the
body of light
But home freezing preserves everything except essence
And if you could make love forever you would
Because the eyes don't like much of the 21st Century
Female beauty is identical to men's in always alighting
upon the thing that it lacks
In Manhattan feeling cold on 8th Avenue looking for
Jackson
And there was somebody with a tool looking inside you
Your shaking his hand and saying *Senor* and then
realizing you were stuffed full of smack
You pray to the Buddha because weak and
insubstantial ones need to look up to something
The Buddha said well you know what he said
And you occasionally test it

And you are doomed if you do because your internal
    flora is in radical imbalance and
You are doomed if you don't because you are
    constitutionally suited to whining
The shit which flows down the Danube builds to a
    mountain outside your front door
If you could ask somebody to stop it you would but
The beloved other and the emperor and all the gods
    just direct you back to your mind
Your mind goes between despair and the need to write
You are in a god-forsaken seaside resort on the east
    coast beneath a stretch of black water
It is clear that your strategies for prosperity return or
    redemption have all failed
The best you can hope for survival is Romanian women
    and Romanian men
Invisibility alternative medicine and a P.O. box a
    functioning typewriter and occasional mail
How many years is it since you last saw your daughter
Prince Far I Echo & the Bunnymen or The Dancing Did
Pete de Freitas & his brother Frank

It was a dark and stormy night and

It is a dark and stormy night and
You do not know if it is January or August
From on top of your kennel
Duty and irresponsibility are all that the artist
  understands to begin with
We who work in photography in small rooms in the
  dark
Photomontage as a weapon in the class struggle
Parties and birthday celebrations
And we photomontage as kind of despairingly inverted
  deathday reflection for men
These days nothing is certain
You can't keep pretending
Everyone loves you as an artist
When you use them in films and you buy them ice
  creams
You thought you were making movies about the
  meaning of life
But all you were doing was projecting your fears and
  desires on to a poorly-lit screen
In the middle of a field with one mouth moving
  indeterminately over another
At the end of a day perhaps to a bored tiny or
  uncomprehending audience
And occasionally you smelled good in the west
You open Casanova's journals and notice his interest in
  everything
His optimism facility with language and ability to make
  the most of carriage travel

But you have to resist

There is no boat for you without holes and there is no
such thing as a benevolent dictator

And when you think about your past lives you are
unable to write

Your wife in one chapter in a different city

And you imagine her opening cockle shells with
enthusiasm

You remember her delight in front of pale urchins and
every day

It becomes more apparent that you will never see her
again

When she was young there were no age spots on her
cheeks or her hands

And she was beautiful in the way of magazines

O it is better now

Poetry satisfying the need for resemblance

You remember the willpower it took every morning to
allow her to sleep

You will never see her again

The love you once had is dispersed

And your children are lost

You do not think this makes you love anyone less

Now everything has the consistency of powder

This is perhaps the greatest and most enduring of facts

If you are reading this letter in a letter

And if you are reading this letter in letter form
Perhaps you can still smell the river's stink
In the weave of the paper in summer
Beside which I write this
It stinking least in August
As it passes parliament on its way to the
Start of the end of the water because
There is an absence in the house in this season of
Recess and in case you do not know it
From the distance at which you are
Reading in time or in miles this man absence is
Whose heart is a mansion looking over a gulag
Whose face is a cube with the surface removed
And whose blocks reach pin fences
This thing to quote myself
With neither beard nor hair trimmed
Is a clock that limits time parting
Only to reappear in ordered cuts
And this thing being deaf to the shadow the sun casts
Is this thing livid to the outskirts of a breeze art
And proof in kind boiled down into a pill of college
  toxins
And wherever this thing lurches
Rock films and pennants of block
This thing filled with calcium in the voids of Eton
Gorged on excrement
Wads the floor with himself
A memory of waters during works
In the ground dreaming ants

If you are reading this in a different century
His memory tentacles
Staples through a hill shrinking ekes
Everything sadder as a result of this it is
Harder to be human
His cup breaking magnets
The way that glue sticks to acid
I am writing this letter before the things of force
Force me out of this language in certain spots
Occupied by smoke
I see the light of the planet being sucked and
I see the light of the planet being
Sucked into the blacker dimensions of his head
I see him coming to bite my ball
He is an insect the size of Middlesex
A vast beach filled with oil-covered bodies
Shitting himself upon the ceiling
Only appearing to finger children
With his thick blue fingers
The one in the middle splitting
Him covered with flag noise and handwriting
His posture composed of failure devoured by flattery
In front of an engine before dressing
His memory average with chickens
If you are reading this letter in disbelief and
If you are on this planet
Without his felt over the period in shreds and bubbles
Consider yourself lucky in this lifetime
His appearance contaminates
Toast hair liquid plaster old paintings
dreams codfish pleading clinks blood

leaps burn dressing ties hours and barbers
Is it any good to offer resistance through meditation
It is
The author function reduced to a whisper
In the presence of milk
Every time that I think of this
Johnson I see a hole the size of an orange
Coughing into the labyrinth

If you are an Italian in London in Summer and

If you are an Italian in London in A.D. 15 or 2018
And you find yourself unsighted in a dark place close
    to public transport
It is better to be in Italy speaking Italian when the
    blows reign down
Or they ship you to hospitals run by Richard Branson
    for cash
Perhaps someone filmed you bleeding on YouTube
You get likes on some websites on the ground where no
    one is
Looking at the leg or the blood or the bag or the arm
There is a foreign body out on the ground
And there is a foreign body out in the English
Night there are foreign bodies occupying English
    ground space
Most often cloud-covered
Where you marched with the people on the march
You thought you were in favour of
Ordinary people and their feet and their ability to
    change things
But you are no longer sure
You were reading Nazim Hikmet's prison writings to his
    wife
And you can do the math concerning the balance
    between the fuckers and the fucked
Their increase and the difference for there is none
    between both
It is useful to laugh about falling off and it is useful to
    hide

Your enemies have stopped
Complaining in the capital about skin colour or accent
    because
In a dark place close to public transport this is England
And it is a Thursday and the weekend is coming
You go out and you go out of your body a little
There is a man and a woman
They were never Italian
This is a free country
It says in The Daily Mail
And it says on the newsfeeds
And it says in the office
It is good in the night on hearing what you think might
    be Italian
To dance your way out of this ignorance and distress
It is good to be white pill'd up and Viking and
It is good to believe what the newspapers write
    wherever you go
It says the same thing in Turkey Germany Hungary
    Poland the South of France Asturias Croatia Bilerus
    Japan
Italy or the Baltic States
Is it good to go out
Among the foreigners in your own country
And find them
Is it good to go out among the foreigners in your own
    country
And find them in a dark place close to public transport
Is it good to go out among the foreigners in your own
    country and find them
A little in love

Feeling good
Go out clubbing at night

For Diana: London: VIII.2018

There comes a time often in airports when you realize that

Even if you love what you want more than you love
  what you have got
There comes a time when you realize that you'll never
  get what you want
Walking around in a landscape that approximates the
  emperor's head
Is enough to fill you with loathing
You realize that your poetry powers only work over
  slogans
You have to use signs to indicate your desires in exile
What sometimes occasions surprise is why nature does
  not cause the sea to grow bigger reading Lucretius
Remembering a poem by Terrance Hayes written in the
  form of a crime report
There is a difference between waving your arms to
  communicate
And your disappearance from the continent
There will come a time when your standing up will or
  will not be enough
It happens that the earth more often threatens a
  collapse than executes it
In spite of the Blackshirts
You think you are forgotten or anonymous in this exile
  looking out from your nest
You think of J-Lo and Bo-Jo and Sho-Bo and
Laughing with Jeff
You thought that once it was your job in the old days of
  language to resist

But all you would do was click to protest
And there were times when you could occasionally
    breathe out
And your cells were not going wild having turned off
    their regulatory clocks
It was good to dive into fountains and be an Italian
Not abused by racists at night and the rivers of blood
    meaning
Everywhere you look white men are sounding off
You are one of them
Sounding off
And the plates beneath the oceans and
The plates in Asia Minor will not stop you from knowing
    that the answer is
To just sit with focus and good intent
And look out at the sea filled with children stopped
    from crossing the sea
By other Italians and the fascists in other countries and
    their police
And the Buddha fields are lined up with them
The way that your head moves from contrition to
    compassion to detachment
And each position is wrong
Even if you love what you have more than you love
    what you want
It is the 21st Century and the planet is full to
    overflowing
I am in love with your beautiful poems
And they come out in various countries in various
    editions
And I kiss your face or at least

I imagine that I kiss your face
Because of this or not because of this
I mean we
Are still lovers in love with everything for what else can
we do
Every time you put your foot down
His chest hair covers the world like a carpet

However broken you feel by nationalists beneath the stars

Your lungs fill with neon once more and you wonder
If you too have lacked grace and elegance
Because you were human when attending to your
  inclinations
On Bredon Hill you had some
And an interest in oriental literature (all of it)
Encircled by spies pilgrims journalists cosmic spheres
  and flashcards
Imagining sonnets as containers substances and states
You move at last to move your arms against the
  government
And like a Vandal and a Goth
Deface records and tapes
In order to escape by means of dabs noz or vape
You imagine your lungs filling with Black Sea water
Once and once only you were made love to
In Paris in summer and for this reason alone
You do not have to apologize for anything
Even though it is true that
Then as now
You did lack the following
Control over sonnets
Elegance and grace

The question that comes up in the poetry test

Concerns something you did not get back then
When you were famous if you knew what the answer
   was
That was the question you were never asked
Concerning sex or race
It not coming up in the Cambridge School of Business
   School
Poetry Test
Fear is the equal of function and the business is the
   business
Upon a map covered with arrows weighing up your
   impact
Now you know that
Every day at 5AM there are people sweeping in
Sweeping in corridors while you are sleeping
And they are paid less than you hand out in pocket
   money to your innumerable kids
And at some point you go swimming
Which indicates how late you are and your position as
   an arriviste
In the interview you remember how not to cross your
   legs
And you picture your body surrounded by light
And there is a book ahead of you because there
   always is
There is a need to apologize for all of the above
Not just because you say there is
You are peaceful in traffic and when you breathe
You feel good underwater having practiced

How to be effective with humans even
Though your base of operations was always founded
    upon vulnerability and stress
Because all poetry is a kind of exile
And because all poetry is a kind of acknowledgement
    of exile
From agency
You liken its impact to an unanswered question and you
    bend over
And you do not know what will happen next
But you know that there is a book ahead of you
Because you say there is and because it is all you have
    left
You watch your back because everyone should watch
    their back
You look forward to the future with impossible hope
For what else you could do
Every day every night
You insert yourself into Blaise Cendrars' arm space
And you ask it to write

And you get out of bed

And you get out of bed in the middle of the night
Or you get out of bed in the darkness before dawn
Or you get out of bed having barely slept but not
   knowing that fact
And you are suddenly awake and you want to read
   something
But you are not really awake and you do not
   remember what it is
Or if it was a book that you read or had written you
   know
You will never find it in your room in the dark beside
   the wine dark sea in a different language
You will never find it because you are an anonymous
   writer and your books have been buried
And you are a famous writer who is incontinent both
In exile from every moment which you felt was
   important
And perhaps you cannot see your hand in front of your
   face
Because of the darkness or because of your age or
   because of the times that you find yourself in
You have your feet at the ends of your body and you
   have something which
When you were horizontal at times you told yourself
   was genius
The ability to read everything in the West and the
   ability to love it without complication or
With complication and feel empowered by your ability
   to hold that contradiction

And now you are awake in a room with and without the
    western canon
And you are awake and the darkness and the absence
    of books
You would give anything to see your beloved's breath
    on your shape but it is impossible
And you would find your daughter in innumerable
    volumes
Night wraps the sky in tribute from the stars there are
    no longer any pills
And they are tearing down the social housing close to
    the water to build waterfront apartments
You cannot see them in the dark but you can feel them
    coming
The sea pulls back again and the sea pulls back to
    sleep
And you can feel them coming for you but they are a
    different them and the coming is a different one
And you read a book about being a father and all you
    want is to be
One of those ordinary characters in a Scandinavian
    novel in an ordinary room
You loved *for colored girls* by Ntozake Shange and
    when you were alive
You were reading about the pointlessness of life and
    you were smoking it all up
And every day is so beautiful you once thought if you
    can see it in the future
And every day will be so beautiful in the past
Standing in a room in the dark
Without books you have nothing but one called

Sadness and without books you have and do not have
    a poetics of space
There is no intertextuality and the reading of Roman
    poetry
There is no way of understanding music and what
The world becomes if it was not designed to culminate
    in a book
And you get out of bed and you do not tread on the
    haiku concerning your wife
And you stand there in the room
There is no other space you can hold it in
Because you have so many things still to say and have
    nothing to write
The books you send out disappear or come back
And your voice can no longer feel your hand in the
    dark
You are no longer a man or a woman or a thing
Because there is no silhouette to reflect or pick out
You think of yourself and then you do not think of
    yourself
As any random selection of nouns placed alongside
    any random number of verbs
You are everything that ever existed slipping
And now that the books have turned themselves into
    nothing
In the blackness there is only the angle of the planet
And it is the one number against which you become a
    different fact
How hard it is in the night with no books
And how hard it is in the night with these things
    whatever they are you know

It doesn't matter
If there was a gypsy ensemble which you saw or
    imagined
Or a salad on a table next to a different salad
You do not have the apparatus to pass the meaning
    you desire through the fluid of your eyeball
And what little sound ever approaches a larger one
    leaves you
Soon you will be a writer without eyes and no sound
Your antennae and your wings and your tape measure
Here they all are in the middle of the night in this
    volume
And here they all are in the middle of the night
In this imaginary volume in this imaginary night
You worked so hard to make yourself invisible in
All your best-selling volumes on poetic imagination and
    reverie
You pretended to be all of the pronouns
And you pretended not to be drunk and you
    pretended to not be in love
But you weren't
And you wrote it or you read it or you thought it
Everything always in a volume called *Paris Stories*
And everything in the stars and the oceans and the
    night and the garbage
Arranging things and calling it the human condition in
    the history of the world
And there is no such thing except suffering
And there is no greater aim than its alleviation
In parks and in corridors and circuses

You read all these things in bedrooms and workshops
    and libraries
And the moment you get out of bed you stand there
    you
Stand there if you touched the doors or the walls
In the history of the world everything human
And in the history of the world nothing inhuman
There is nothing smaller or bigger or bigger or smaller
    than ever you realize
One rises to address
In hours like these at the end of your life
You and me fading
The ages history and all creation
At the end of your book
    ot the heart
    of the night

I spit on my passport

. . .

Not a word of death

Marina Tsvetaeva

photo: Jess Robson

Tim Atkins has been a member of the summer faculty at The Jack Kerouac School of Disembodied Poetics at Naropa University, and a member of Carla Harryman's Poets Theatre in San Francisco. He is the author of many books, including *Atkins Collected Petrarch* (a Times Literary Supplement and Salon.com book of the year), *Deep Osaka* (a photobook), *Koto Y Yo* (all from Crater Press), *25 Sonnets* (The Figures), *Petrarch* (Book Thug), *Horace* (O Books) and a collaboration with his daughter, Yuki Lily Matsubayashi Atkins, *A Girl Is A Machine Made Of Birds* (Canary Woof Press). He is also the author of a play: *The World's Furious Song Flows Through My Skirt* (Stoma Press) and a novel *The Bath-Tub* (forthcoming from Boiler House Press). He also wrote the introduction to *breth: the collected-selected poems of bill bissett,* published by Talon. He has read and performed his work in the Houses of Parliament (for Pussy Riot), in concert at the Victoria & Albert Museum, and all over North America and Europe. His work has been translated into Spanish, Japanese, Catalan, French, and Lithuanian. *Mother*—a collaborative film-poem made with Graeme Maguire was a finalist at the Cyclop International Videopoetry Festival and at the Rabbit Heart Film festival in 2014. Poems have appeared in many anthologies, including *The Penguin Book of the Prose Poem* (2018) *The Reality Street Book of the Sonnet*, and Faber's *The Thunder Mutters* (edited by Alice Oswald). The founder and editor of the long-running international online poetry journal, *onedit*, Tim works in the Creative Writing programme at the University of Roehampton.